To

From

Date

On the Path with God

Text Copyright © 2011 by Erwin Lutzer

Artwork Copyright © 2011 Scanlan Windows to the World, by John and Debora Scanlan for International Artist Management Group Inc.

Published by Harvest House Publishers
Eugene, Oregon 97402
www.harvesthousepublishers.com

ISBN 978-0-7369-3936-2

Design and production by Left Coast Design, Portland, Oregon

This book was inspired by a message on Enoch, which I heard many years ago. It was given by one of my seminary professors, Dr. S. Lewis Johnson, who faithfully walked with God and saw the end of his distinguished earthly career in 2004.

Printed in China

11 12 13 14 15 16 17 18 19 / IM / 10 9 8 7 6 5 4 3 2 1

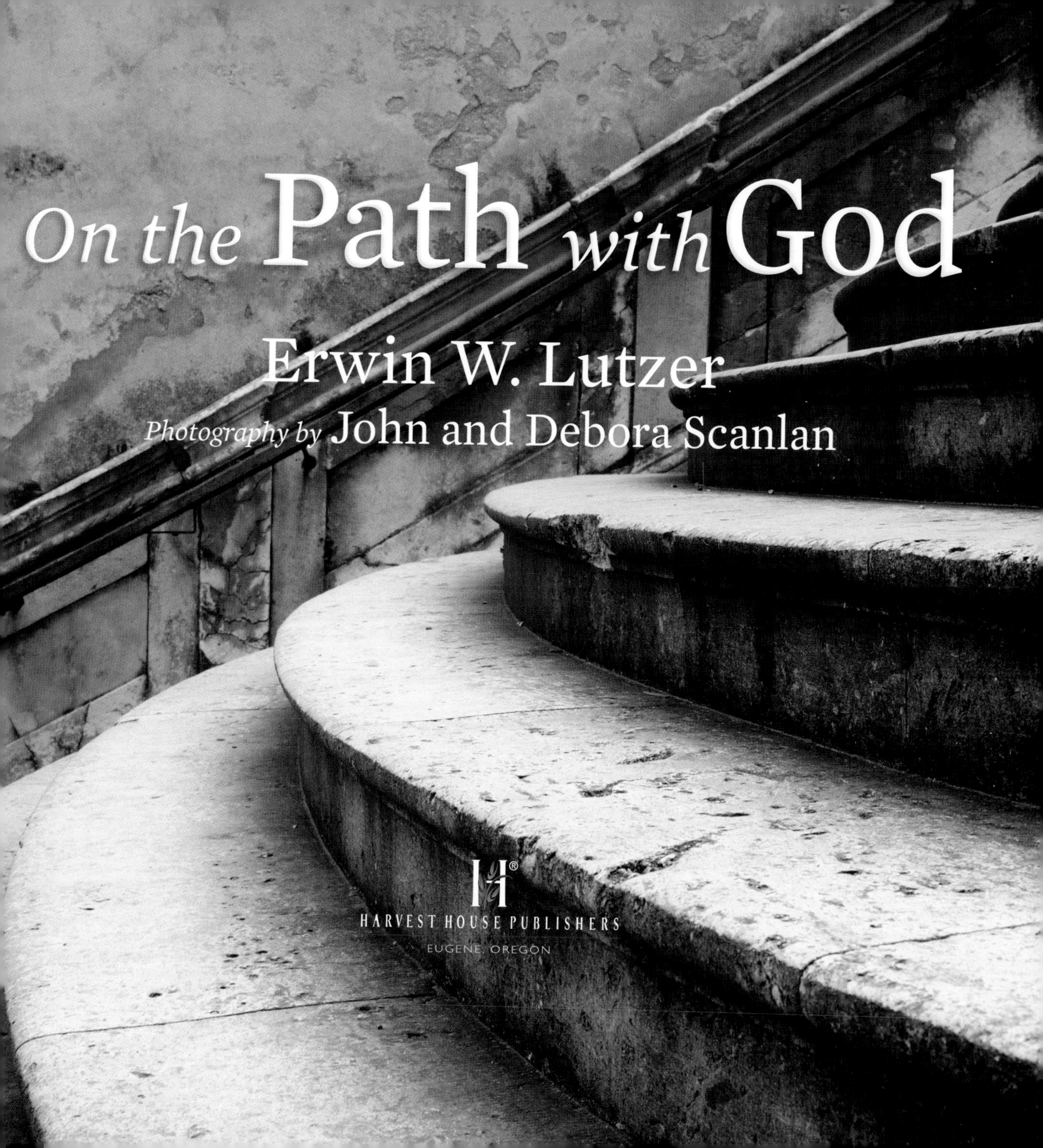

On the Path with God

Erwin W. Lutzer

Photography by John and Debora Scanlan

H®
HARVEST HOUSE PUBLISHERS
EUGENE, OREGON

✦ DEDICATION ✦

To my father and mother, Gustav and Wanda Lutzer, who, like Enoch, having walked with God for many years, left a legacy of faithfulness for generations to come. My father entered into the presence of the Lord at the age of 106; my godly mother is still living at the age of 102. "As God has said: 'I will live with them and walk among them, and I will be their God, and they will be my people'" (2 Corinthians 6:16).

$$\diamond\diamond\diamond\diamond\diamond$$

✦ CONTENTS ✦

❈ FROM MY HEART TO YOURS ❈

Life has become so complicated. Do you feel it too? Each stride we make toward simplicity by adopting technological helps, minute-by-minute planners, and the advice of efficiency experts sets us on a pace that can be even more stressful. Too many priorities vie for our time, our hearts, and our lives. And we get lost.

Thankfully God has reduced what is most important to a simple statement found in Micah 6:8: "He has shown you, O mortal, what is good. And what does the LORD require of you? To act justly and to love mercy and to walk humbly with your God."

My prayer is that you and I will be able to focus on this single goal: to walk humbly with God, and experience the increase of joy and strength that this walk, this relationship with God brings to our journey.

Dr. Erwin Lutzer
Moody Church, Chicago

———————— ◇◇◇◇ ————————

Come, descendants of Jacob, let us walk in the light of the LORD.

Isaiah 2:5

My steps have held to your paths;
my feet have not stumbled.
I call on you, my God, for you will answer me;
turn your ear to me and hear my prayer.

Psalm 17:5-6

WHY WALK WITH GOD?

When Jesus spoke again to the people, he said,
"I am the light of the world. Whoever follows me will
never walk in darkness, but will have the light of life."

John 8:12

A tour through a cemetery can be beneficial and educational. I like to read epitaphs because they often say something interesting about the person who is finished with this life and has gone on to the next. Maybe epitaphs should be required reading for everyone once a year. They are a reminder that life is short and that eternity is near.

Most epitaphs are serious, some are tragic, and yes, there are at least a few that are funny. I'm told that this poem is found on the tombstone of a lady named Anna Wallace in England:

The children of Israel wanted bread.
The Lord sent them manna.
Old clerk Wallace wanted a wife.
The devil sent him Anna.

Here is a poem I learned in grade school, though I doubt it is on a tombstone —it could be. It contains an important message about automobile safety:

Here lies the body of William Jay,
Who died while maintaining his right
of way.
He was right, completely right as he
sped along,
But he's just as dead as if he'd been
wrong!

My favorite epitaph is found in the Bible, embedded in a long list of genealogies in the fifth chapter of Genesis. To read these verses is like walking through

I would rather walk with God
in the dark than go alone
in the light.

MARY GARDINER BRAINARD

a cemetery. The names are difficult to pronounce and we are left to guess what life was like so many centuries ago. Like the tolling of a bell, every tombstone bears the same message; six times we read the simple phrase "and he died."

Then unexpectedly we discover that there was a man who did not die! His name was Enoch, and of him we read in verse 24, "Enoch walked faithfully with God; then he was no more, because God took him away." Twice we are told that Enoch "walked with God." In fact, he walked with God right into heaven!

This epitaph is perhaps one of the most beautiful phrases in the entire Bible. If it could be said of you and me that we "walked with God," nothing more need be said. Those few words contain an eternity of meaning.

The feeling remains that God is on the journey, too.

TERESA OF AVILA

AN INVITATION TO THE JOURNEY

Walking with God is both difficult and simple. Difficult because it takes thought, discipline, and commitment; simple because the same characteristics that apply to walking with a close friend or a loved one apply to walking with God.

Enoch walked with God in the midst of a society filled with temptations and obstacles just like those we face. He is a powerful reminder that we can be faithful to walk with God in our day as well. When we accept the invitation to begin the journey, trials and distractions need not keep us from our time with the Almighty.

Interestingly, Enoch was motivated to begin this journey after his first son, Methuselah, was born. Maybe he felt a new sense of responsibility as he held the baby boy in his arms. Perhaps as the child reached out to touch the stubble of his father's beard Enoch said to himself, "I need to reorder my priorities and begin to take God more seriously." Evidently he realized that the greatest contribution he could make in life was to guide his family on the right path.

Spend some moments reflecting on what motivates your heart to walk with the Lord today.

The joy of the LORD is your strength.

Nehemiah 8:10

Have you faced a trial and found yourself ready to give your sorrow to God? Do you long to leave a legacy of faith for your children? Maybe you've been in fellowship with the Lord for many years and you are ready for refreshment. Together we can explore how to walk with God and embrace the meaningful, remarkable, and abundant life He has planned for you. Let's take a step forward toward the light of life.

You have declared this day that the LORD is your God and that you will walk in obedience to him, that you will keep his decrees, commands and laws — that you will listen to him. And the LORD has declared this day that you are his people, his treasured possession as he promised, and that you are to keep all his commands.

Deuteronomy 26:17-18

❋ HELP FOR THE JOURNEY ❋

I've often thought about what others might say of me after I die. I don't mean the beautiful eulogies often given at funerals. Instead, I wonder what people will really think—what they will *really* remember about the impact for good or ill I have had in their lives. God, of course, will give the final evaluation, but imagine our legacy if it could be said that we "walked with God."

➤ If an epitaph were written for you today, what would it be? Are you satisfied with that? What do you hope you will be remembered for?

➤ Consider Jesus' simple invitation to brothers Simon and Andrew referenced below. Think about how wonderful it feels to have Jesus call to you today in the same, simple way. What is your response to Jesus as He waves to you and says, "Come, follow me"?

> As Jesus walked beside the Sea of Galilee, he saw Simon and his brother Andrew casting a net into the lake, for they were fishermen. "Come, follow me," Jesus said, "and I will make you fishers for people."
>
> **Mark 1:16-17**

➤ God provides what you need each step of the way. What worries or weaknesses do you want to give to God—*need* to give to God—in exchange for His hope and renewing strength?

> Even youths grow tired and weary, and young men stumble and fall;
> but those who hope in the Lord will renew their strength.
> They will soar on wings like eagles;
> they will run and not grow weary,
> they will walk and not be faint.
>
> **Isaiah 40:30-31**
>
> Your word is a lamp for my feet, a light on my path.
>
> **Psalm 119:105**

WALKING WITH GOD
CREATES FELLOWSHIP

The LORD your God is the one who goes with
you. He will not fail you or forsake you.

Deuteronomy 31:6 NASB

D o two walk together unless they have agreed to do so?" is a question posed by the ancient prophet Amos. The obvious answer is no, they cannot. Or at least they can't *enjoy* walking with each other as long as there are "issues" between them. Just try walking with someone with whom you have just had an argument.

Those of us who are married understand how difficult it is to walk united with our spouse after an unresolved dispute. Just last week I spoke to a woman who had an argument with her husband in a restaurant. When they walked onto the street, she took her wedding ring and flung it as far as she could. That night, to no one's surprise, they parted ways; one went west, the other east. (No, they never did find the ring!)

An argument can keep us apart, but so will differing pursuits. My wife, Rebecca, and I often start out walking together in a mall, but at some point we part ways when she chooses to walk into a clothes store while I find my way to a bookstore. We love each other, but we are different people with different interests.

Walking with God means that there is complete agreement between us and the Almighty. We never have to walk away from God because of different interests— God is interested in everything that is

> Love is an image of God,
> and not a lifeless image, but the
> living essence of the divine nature
> which beams full of all goodness.
>
> **MARTIN LUTHER**

good and wholesome for us! However, when we harbor sin in our hearts, we will part ways; or at least we will no longer be aware of His presence. When we choose our own path, He is grieved because He loves us and cares about our lives and future. He stays with us when we stray, but our experience of His blessing fades.

AGREEING WITH GOD

First John 1:9 promises that "if we confess our sins, he is faithful and just and will forgive us our sins and purify us from all unrighteousness." The word "confess" means to "agree with." When I confess, I am saying, "God, I agree that this is sin; I agree that I need forgiveness, and I also agree that You have the right to take this out of my life." We are submitting to God and seeking

Blessed are those who have learned to acclaim you, who walk in the light of your presence, LORD.

Psalm 89:15

to be in spiritual agreement with Him.

Here is a remarkable, wonderful truth. The apostle John writes that we as Christians should have fellowship with one another and then he adds in 1 John 1:3: "And our fellowship is with the Father and with his Son, Jesus Christ." It is not just that we have fellowship with each other, but *God also has fellowship with us!*

First John 1:7 states, "If we walk in the light, as he is in the light, we have fellowship with one another, and the blood of Jesus, his Son, purifies us from all sin." Isn't it wonderful and reassuring to know that God takes pleasure in this walk with us? When "we walk in the light, as he is in the light," it means that we are constantly walking with our lives open to God; we

agree with Him about everything that He brings to our attention. We no longer see our lives as belonging to ourselves but belonging to Him. We are in complete agreement as we head into our days walking alongside the One who is with us today, tomorrow, and forever.

This is love: that we walk in obedience to his
commands. As you have heard from the beginning,
his command is that you walk in love.

2 John 1:6

✤ HELP FOR THE JOURNEY ✤

Giving to God every part of yourself and seeking His leading in all areas of life is an ongoing part of this wonderful relationship. Every day there are new needs, concerns, or trouble areas that you can bring to God as you walk with Him. It is a great joy to have fellowship with the Lord.

As I've grown in my relationship with God, I spend more time submitting to—and worshipping—God than I do in voicing my requests. Create an unforgettable walk with the Lord by following these simple steps:

➤ Spend time in prayer and give to God all that stands between you and your agreement with Him. Continue your walk with refreshed connection.

➤ What does fellowship with the Almighty bring to your life right now? What strength and sense of hope have you received from Him in the past?

➤ Read and consider memorizing these compelling commands and ask God for the strength to live your life in agreement with them.

I urge you, brothers and sisters, in view of God's mercy, to offer your bodies as living sacrifices, holy and pleasing to God—this is your true and proper worship. Do not conform to the pattern of this world, but be transformed by the renewing of your mind. Then you will be able to test and approve what God's will is—his good, pleasing and perfect will.

Romans 12:1-2

Follow God's example, therefore, as dearly loved children and walk in the way of love, just as Christ loved us and gave himself up for us as a fragrant offering and sacrifice to God.

Ephesians 5:1-2

They heard the sound of the Lord God walking in the garden in the cool of the day.

Genesis 3:8 NKJV

WALKING WITH GOD HELPS YOU MAKE PROGRESS

Walk in obedience to all that the LORD your God has commanded you, so that you may live and prosper and prolong your days in the land that you will possess.

Deuteronomy 5:33

I don't particularly enjoy my exercise cycle, even though I use it with some degree of regularity; the problem is that no matter how fast I peddle, the scenery never changes. I begin at point A and end at point A. I'd rather take a jog in a park or walk along a beach. When I walk I want to go somewhere; if I begin at point A, I would like to arrive at point B and C. I enjoy progress.

When you go on a stroll with a friend, you stay in step so that you can talk and enjoy making progress together. But a walk with children is a different experience, isn't it? Our children seldom stayed in step with Rebecca and me as we strolled on the sidewalk. They either lagged behind or ran ahead. Lagging behind gave them a chance to see the sights at their own pace, and running ahead gave them the exhilaration of pretending to have won a race.

Staying in step with God involves practice and sensitivity. We should neither be anxious to run ahead, nor should we be so timid as to lag behind.

In the Gospels, we find Peter making both mistakes in the same evening. In John 18:10-11 we find that he ran ahead of Jesus and took his sword and whacked

> In the morning, prayer is the key that opens to us the treasure of God's mercies and blessings; in the evening, it is the key that shuts us up under his protection and safeguard.
>
> **HENRY WARD BEECHER**

off the ear of the servant of the high priest when some people came to arrest Jesus. Jesus rebuked Peter, saying, "Put your sword away! Shall I not drink the cup the Father has given me?" Then later the same night, Peter walked too slowly when Jesus was taken into custody. Mark 14:54 reads, "Peter followed him at a distance." Self-will made him get ahead of Jesus and fear made him lag behind.

Even the disciples struggled to stay alongside Jesus! So how can we strive to keep pace faithfully?

STAY IN STEP WITH GOD

The more devotion we have to God the better we can stay in step with Him. In short, staying in step means that we are, to the best of our knowledge, in His will, doing what He designed us to do. I have a friend who prays every morning, "Lord, when I lay my head on the pillow tonight might I be able to say I served You to the best of my ability."

Recently someone asked me if walking with God became easier as the years went by. I answered, "Yes, my faith and confidence in God continue to grow, but so do the mysteries of God's ways!" There is much about God we do not know, but the longer we walk with Him the more sure-footed we become as we walk along our daily path.

D.L. Moody, who founded the Moody Church and Moody Bible Institute, was a great evangelist, but he was also a humble man who sought God with all of his heart. He knew that he could progress in his walk with God only if he had regular time in the presence of the Almighty by reading the Bible and praying. His words offer great wisdom and encouragement for us:

> A man can no more take in a supply of grace for the future than he can eat enough for the next six months or take sufficient air into his lungs at one time to sustain life for a week. We must draw upon God's boundless store of grace from day to day as we need it.

Progress means that we begin each morning making sure that our very first step is taken in the right direction. In fact, our walk begins even before we get out of bed; in those few moments as we anticipate our day, we are deciding who we will follow and how.

Remember, LORD, how I have walked before you faithfully and with wholehearted devotion and have done what is good in your eyes.

2 Kings 20:3

✤ HELP FOR THE JOURNEY ✤

rogress begins with having a quiet time in the morning. If you are not in the habit of beginning the day with God, start by getting out of bed 15-30 minutes earlier than usual. You'll be surprised how refreshed you'll feel after this becomes a part of your daily living. Don't worry; God will make up the "lost" time for you! Here is a plan you can follow:

➢ Pray before you get out of bed: Soon after I awaken, I pray, "Today, Lord, glorify Yourself at my expense." And then I add a short prayer affirming that I intend to walk in the Spirit throughout the day, in total dependence on Him.

➢ After you are out of bed, read a chapter of the Bible, answering three questions: *First*, what does this passage teach me about God? *Second*, is there a promise I must believe? And *finally*, is there a command I must obey? When you close your Bible you should have at least one clear idea that you can meditate on all day.

➢ Pray Scripture: Choose a familiar passage, perhaps Psalm 23. Now pray the passage, inserting your name or the name of a family member. "Lord, I pray today that Susan might delight to be Your sheep and to want nothing as much as she desires You. Thank You that You provide for her; keep her from fear and lead her in paths of righteousness for Your name's sake..."

After you have prayed some of the psalms, graduate to the prayers in the epistles of Paul (for example, Ephesians 1:15-23; 3:14-21; Colossians 1:9-14; and so on). You can also pray these prayers for your children or grandchildren. You'll discover that when you begin your morning with God, you will remain conscious of His presence throughout the whole day. You will move from point A to point B and point C.

Show me your ways, Lord, teach me your paths. Guide me in your truth and teach me, for you are God my Savior, and my hope is in you all day long.

Psalm 25:4-5

Trust in the Lord with all your heart and lean not on your own understanding; in all your ways submit to him, and he will make your paths straight.

Proverbs 3:5-6

WALKING WITH GOD
BUILDS TRUST

Whoever dwells in the shelter of the Most High will rest in the shadow of the Almighty. I will say of the Lord, "He is my refuge and my fortress, my God, in whom I trust."

Psalm 91:1-2

When our grandson, Samuel, was about five years old, I took him for a walk in a forest preserve, complete with hidden trails and a winding river. As we turned onto a path to return home, he said, "No, Papa, this is the wrong way. We have to go home over here!"

And he pointed to a path that led in the opposite direction. "No, Samuel, this is the path. You have to trust me," I said with confidence. Reluctantly he walked toward me, kicking the sand with the stub of his shoes. "But Papa, it is so hard to trust!"

We were in a forest preserve where I'd walked for years; I not only knew the trail we were on, but I could already see the roof of our condo above the treetops.

Then I thought of how God knows all the paths in our lives. He knows not only where they lead, through the hills and the valleys, but also where they will eventually take us. And yet Samuel was right—*it is so hard to trust!* Even when the one we are following can see ahead.

It is easy to walk with God in the sunshine when we are healthy, we have money, and our family is doing well. In fact, in such times, we even think we might not need His companionship because everything is under control. So because trust does not come naturally to us, God leads us into those dark times in our lives when we become desperate and we are *forced* to trust Him.

> Grace is but glory begun, and glory is but grace perfected.
>
> **JONATHAN EDWARDS**

GOD SEES YOUR NEED

When the disciples were in the middle of a fierce storm on the Sea of Galilee, they lost all hope. At four in the morning, they were exhausted and scared. In the darkness they were not able to see Jesus, and their trust in Him was fading with each crashing wave. And although they could not see Him, He could see them and came to where they were by walking on the water.

Even in times of darkness, when we cannot see God, He can see us and comes to us in our need. How has God come to you during your darkest storm?

> The gatekeeper opens the gate for him,
> and the sheep listen to his voice. He calls
> his own sheep by name and leads them out.
> When he has brought out all his own, he
> goes on ahead of them, and his sheep
> follow him because they
> know his voice.
>
> **John 10:3-4**

> Through the dark and stormy night
> Faith beholds a feeble light
> Up the blackness streaking;
> Knowing God's own time is best,
> In a patient hope I rest.
> For the full day-breaking!
>
> **JOHN GREENLEAF WHITTIER**

❧ HELP FOR THE JOURNEY ❧

How do we learn to trust in God's faithfulness with every bit of our being and for every aspect of our lives? God wants us to walk with Him in the sunshine so we will be better prepared to trust Him in the darkness of our unanswered questions and seemingly pointless pain. There is an old saying, "Never doubt in the darkness what you have learned in the light."

➤ Increase your trust in God. Trust is developed as you grow in confidence that God is in charge, and He has your best interests in mind. Can you release control of your goals; your family's well-being; your health, dreams, and decisions? This is the beginning of discovering God's faithfulness!

➤ Suffering can drive us away from God. But when we rest in God's faithfulness, He will use our suffering to draw us closer to Him. Speaker and author Joni Eareckson Tada, who became a quadriplegic after a diving accident many years ago, offers this wisdom: "Suffering is God increasing our capacity to experience more of Christ." Experience more of Christ in whatever trial you are facing.

➤ Finally, let us follow the example of Jesus, who submitted His will to the Father and agreed with Him even at great personal cost. "Going a little farther, he fell with his face to the ground and prayed, 'My Father, if it is possible, may this cup be taken from me. Yet not as I will, but as you will'" (Matthew 26:39).

This I call to mind and therefore I have hope: Because of the LORD's great love we are not consumed, for his compassions never fail. They are new every morning; great is your faithfulness.

Lamentations 3:21-23

WALKING WITH GOD
BRINGS HONOR

I will walk among you and be your God, and you will be my people.

Leviticus 26:12

◇◇◇◇◇

Who would you like to be seen walking with? One day at a professional baseball game, I watched as boys flocked around their favorite players. They hounded them for autographs and had their pictures taken standing right next to their heroes. They felt exhilaration and honor just to be seen with those they admired.

My personal hero was not a sports superstar, but the famous evangelist Billy Graham. Ever since I was a teenager, I not only admired Mr. Graham, but followed his ministry and even tried to preach as he did! Then in 1988 he came to Moody Church for a rally, and I spent some time with him in my study. You can be sure I did not mind having my picture taken with him as a small crowd gathered at the bottom of the stairs as we walked down together. To be seen "walking with Billy" had been a lifelong dream.

I once read a story about a young investment broker who was a personal friend of Lord Rothschild in London. He visited the famous financier in his office and complained, "Mr. Rothschild, I'm not getting any business. I wonder if you can help me." Rothschild replied, "Let's take a walk around the London Stock Exchange." So together they walked around the Exchange; then they returned to the office. As the young man was leaving, he said, "Well, I hope

---

◇◇◇◇◇

Reputation is what men and women think of us; character is what God and angels know of us.

THOMAS PAINE

◇◇◇◇◇

29

We can easily
manage, if we will
only take, each
day, the burden
appointed for it.
But the load will
be too heavy for
us if we carry
yesterday's burden
over again today,
and then add the
burden of the
morrow to the
weight before we
are required to
bear it.

JOHN NEWTON

I run in the path
of your commands,
for you have broad-
ened my under-
standing.
Psalm 119:32

you can help me sometime." And Rothschild replied, "I already have."

After that, the young man had as much business as he could handle! He'd been seen walking with Rothschild, which was all he needed to increase his stature and popularity!

BEING SEEN WITH GOD

Of course we want to walk with our heroes. But do they want to walk with us? An aspiring basketball star wants to walk with Michael Jordan, but does Michael Jordan want to walk with him? Incredibly, God is willing to be seen with us; He is willing to walk with us in the day-to-day experiences of life. That we would walk with Him is His idea, not ours! "As God has said:

A grateful thought toward heaven
is of itself a prayer.

GOTTHOLD EPHRAIM LESSING

'I will live with them *and walk among them*, and I will be their God, and they will be my people" (2 Corinthians 6:16). God comes alongside of us and says, "Let's walk together."

We and God are members of the same family, "Both the one who makes men holy and those who are made holy are of the same family. So Jesus is not ashamed to call them brothers and sisters" (Hebrews 2:11). I've known many families in which one sibling is ashamed of another; the good son does not want to be associated with his wayward brother. Yet Jesus is not ashamed to call us

His brothers and sisters; He enjoys being our companion on the road of life.

The LORD God is a sun and shield; the LORD bestows favor and honor;

no good thing does he withhold from those whose walk is blameless.

Psalm 84:11

⊹ HELP FOR THE JOURNEY ⊹

Begin each day with the assurance that you are walking side-by-side with God. You'll notice a new sense of joy overflowing through your thoughts, actions, dreams, and decisions. This is the great delight of living with your identity in Christ.

➤ Have you ever longed to be seen with someone? What quality, status, or stature did that person possess that you wanted to be associated with? How does walking with God give you a sense of honor and value?

➤ Take time to consider the present honors that come to those who walk with God. Let us consider what we can enjoy today if we belong to Christ. The following list is taken from Romans chapter 8, a chapter that gives astounding details about our present inheritance:

The honor of forgiveness—"There is now no condemnation for those who are in Christ Jesus...who do not live according to the flesh but according to the Spirit" (Romans 8:1, 14).

The honor of the Holy Spirit—"You, however, are not in the realm of the flesh but are in the realm of the Spirit, if indeed the Spirit of God lives in you. And if anyone does not have the Spirit of Christ, they do not belong to Christ" (Romans 8:9).

The honor of Sonship—"The Spirit you received does not make you slaves, so that you live in fear again; rather, the Spirit you received brought about your adoption to sonship. And by him we cry, 'Abba, Father'" (Romans 8:15).

The honor of heirship—"The Spirit himself testifies with our spirit that we are God's children. Now if we are children, then we are heirs—heirs of God and co-heirs with Christ, if indeed we share in his sufferings in order that we may also share in his glory" (Romans 8:16-17).

The honor of future victory—"No, in all these things we are more than conquerors through him who loved us" (Romans 8:37).

The honor of unconditional love—"I am convinced that neither death nor life, neither angels nor demons, neither the present nor the future, nor any powers, neither height nor depth, nor anything else in all creation, will be able to separate us from the love of God that is in Christ Jesus our Lord" (Romans 8:38-39).

➤ Pray for awareness of God's leading in areas of honor. As you strive to be Christlike, lift up your prayers of thanksgiving for being able to be seen with God, to be known as one of His children.

WALKING WITH GOD TAKES TIME

Observe the commands of the LORD your God,
walking in obedience to him and revering him.

Deuteronomy 8:6

M y doctor tells me that I should take a brisk walk two or three times a week. But by the time I dress for exercise, take my walk, and then shower, the whole effort can take up an hour or more of my time. Sometimes I am just too busy to go walking.

Similarly, walking with God takes time. And if we don't take the time to rearrange our schedules, we undercut our fellowship with God. When that happens we are less productive, less fulfilled, and less useful. "God works for those who wait for him," said the prophet Isaiah. When we wait for God, time is not lost, but gained.

> God be praised, who, to believing
> souls, gives light in the darkness,
> comfort in despair.
>
> **WILLIAM SHAKESPEARE**

Remember the story of how Martha fretted about preparing a meal when Jesus was in her home, whereas her sister Mary sat at the feet of Jesus and heard His teaching? Mary found the freedom to do what women in her day never did, and that was to sit at the feet of one who was regarded as a rabbi in a public setting. Incredibly, Jesus, contrary to expectations, never questioned her competence to hear His word.

Martha and Mary had the same amount of time—the same number of hours in that house that afternoon. Martha opted for something important in its own right; yet, Mary, God bless her, opted for something even more important—eternally important.

According to Jesus, Mary was using her time more wisely.

Jesus knew that Martha had taken on too much. Martha even asked Jesus to tell Mary to help her. But He didn't. "'Martha, Martha,' the Lord answered, 'you are worried and upset about many things, but few things are needed—or indeed only one. Mary has chosen what is better, and it will not be taken away from her'" (Luke 10:41-42). Jesus was gently reaching out toward Martha's heart. He pointed out that her mind was distracted, divided between her domestic responsibilities and a special passing opportunity. How often have you made the difficult decision of choosing between productivity or investing precious moments of time with a loved one, a child, a stranger in need, or God?

And, when I pray, my heart is in my prayer.

HENRY WADSWORTH LONGFELLOW

THE ONE THING

You will be relieved to know that we do not have to choose between being a Mary or a Martha. It is unrealistic to think that we can spend as much time, say, in Bible reading as we do working a 40- or 50-hour workweek. But we must see our relationship with Jesus extend over and above all of our other kinds of responsibility. We work in fellowship with Jesus; we relate to our family responsibilities in fellowship with Jesus; and we take care of ourselves in fellowship with Jesus.

Jesus is, therefore, always first—in our family, in our vocation, in our service at church.

We have to take time for the "one thing" that is needed. We may have many different things, but there is one thing we must have—one thing that is really necessary!

Imagine that $1,440 is put into your bank account every day. At midnight, whatever portion of that money you have not used will disappear from your account, never to be seen again. This would leave you with these options: (1) You could choose to not spend the money; just let it come into your account and then disappear. (2) You could spend the money frivolously on worthless things. Or (3) you could budget it wisely, choosing to use the money on things that mattered.

With that in mind, remember that God gives you a gift of 1,440 minutes every day. How do you wish to use them?

Teach me your way, LORD, that I may rely on your faithfulness; give me an undivided heart, that I may fear your name.

Psalm 86:11

✤ HELP FOR THE JOURNEY ✤

Without a plan, time is squandered and we can fall victim to the urge of the moment. How do we redeem the time? How do we make the most of our lives?

We must determine what we want our life to become. We must run the race of life with the end results in mind. What changes will you have to make in order for it to be said that you "walked with God"? Ask yourself: What does my schedule show me about the importance of my relationship with God?

➤ Pull from your schedule anything that distracts you from God or that redirects your path away from His priorities for you. Remember, it takes time to be holy. Each day impacts all of eternity.

➤ Designate time to nurture the disciplines of the Christian life. Also add in challenges that will help you become who you should be. Attend a Bible study, an inspirational seminar, or a marriage conference. Volunteer for an organization that you believe in.

> Noah was a righteous man, blameless among the people of his time, and he walked faithfully with God.
>
> **Genesis 6:9**

➤Make personal relationships a high priority. Now is the time to be reconciled to that person whom you have avoided because of an uncomfortable relationship; now is the time to reconnect with your family. Twenty years from now, what will you wish you had done today? Do it *now*.

Test me, LORD, and try me, examine my heart and my mind; for I have always been mindful of your unfailing love and have lived in reliance on your faithfulness.

Psalm 26:2-3

WALKING WITH GOD
HAS ITS REWARDS

You make known to me the path of life; you will fill me with
joy in your presence, with eternal pleasures at your right hand.

Psalm 16:11

⊸◦◇◈◇◦⊸

If about Enoch we read, "Before he was taken, he was commended as one who pleased God" (Hebrews 11:5). Even in his life, he knew that he was pleasing God in his daily walk with the Almighty. We should not be surprised that the next verse reads, "And without faith it is impossible to please God, because anyone who comes to him must believe that he exists and that he rewards those who earnestly seek him." Our reward is to know Him and prove Him faithful in this life.

A reward that rises up as we walk with God is that we have the assurance that we know God and are pleasing to Him. Enoch was "commended as one who pleased God." He knew that his relationship with God was secure and his eternal destiny settled. Centuries later, Jesus defined this eternal life as a personal relationship with the Almighty. "Now this is eternal life: that they may know you, the only true God, and Jesus Christ, whom you have sent" (John 17:3).

> How good is man's life, the mere living!
> How fit to employ all the heart and the
> soul and the senses, forever in joy!
>
> **ROBERT BROWNING**

THE PLEASURE OF THE WALK

The rewards and joys keep coming. When we journey with the Almighty, we become personally fulfilled; we discover the pleasure of delighting in God and in so doing find the reason for our existence. In the process, we experience deep satisfaction: "Take delight in the LORD, and he will give you the desires of your heart" (Psalm 37:4). Thus, in seeking God's pleasure, we actually are seeking our own. I'm confident that Enoch would agree that walking with God gave him great delight and joy.

C.S. Lewis wrote that in the Psalms God is the "all-satisfying Object." His people rejoice in Him for the "exceeding joy" they are given through faith in Him. Peter put it this way: "Though you have not seen him, you love him; and even though you do not see him now, you believe in him and are filled with an inexpressible and glorious joy, for you are receiving the end result of your faith, the salvation of your souls" (1 Peter 1:8-9).

When we walk with God, we are rewarded with both the personal satisfaction of knowing Him and the assurance that we are pleasing to Him.

And now, Israel, what does the LORD your God ask of you but to fear the LORD your God, to walk in obedience to him, to love him, to serve the LORD your God with all your heart and with all your soul, and to observe the LORD's commands and decrees that I am giving you today for your own good?

Deuteronomy 10:12-13

The LORD your God will bless you in all your harvest and in all the work of your hands, and your joy will be complete.

Deuteronomy 16:15

✦ HELP FOR THE JOURNEY ✦

G od's promises stretch the limits of our imagination. These are the assurances given to what the Bible calls "overcomers"—that is, to those who have transferred their trust to Christ and have therefore experienced the new life God gives us.

> This is love for God: to obey his commands. And his commands are not burdensome, for everyone born of God overcomes the world. This is the victory that has overcome the world, even our faith. Who is it that overcomes the world? Only the one who believes that Jesus is the Son of God.
> **1 John 5:3-5**

A taste of the pleasures and rewards of your future destination can be experienced today. As you gain a deeper understanding of God's love for you and have fellowship with Him through valleys and celebrations, you will savor that wonder of walking with God just as Enoch did.

➢ How have you experienced the life of an overcomer? Think about these joys of your inheritance in the life to come. Pay special attention to the emphasis I've added in italics.

> Whoever has ears, let them hear what the Spirit says to the churches. To the one who is victorious, *I will give the right to eat from the tree of life, which is in the paradise of God.*
> **Revelation 2:7**

> To the one who is victorious, *I will give the right to sit with me on my throne, just as I was victorious and sat down with my Father on his throne.*
> **Revelation 3:21**

➢ Is God your "all-satisfying Object"? How is your life different when you place God as the focal point of your heart, soul, and life?

➢ What blessings, insights, and peace have you experienced during even the most difficult portions of your journey when you've lived this way?

WALKING WITH GOD LEADS TO A FINAL DESTINATION

Do not fear, for I am with you; do not anxiously look about you,

for I am your God. I will strengthen you, surely I will help you,

surely I will uphold you with My righteous right hand.

Isaiah 41:10 NASB

You and I were born with an expiration date. Enoch's life on earth ended earlier than he expected, and ours might too. In fact, Enoch went to heaven without dying and, according to the New Testament, a whole generation of believers will do the same. "Listen, I tell you a mystery: We will not all sleep [die], but we will all be changed—in a flash, in the twinkling of an eye, at the last trumpet. For the trumpet will sound, the dead will be raised imperishable, and we will be changed" (1 Corinthians 15:51-52). Paul's point is that when Christ returns the dead in Christ will be raised, but believers who are alive at the time will be instantly transformed into their heavenly bodies without dying. Like Enoch, they will go from this life to the next and by-pass death itself.

And what of our future? Not surprisingly, God's plan is that we keep walking with Him. In Revelation 21:22-24 this scene is described: "I did not see a temple in the city, because the Lord God Almighty and the Lamb are its temple. The city does not need the sun or the moon to shine on it, for the glory of God gives it light, and the Lamb is its lamp. The nations will walk by its light, and the kings of the earth will bring their splendor into it" (Revelation 21:22-24).

In John Bunyan's *Pilgrim's Progress*, two men named Christian and Hopeful

> Hope is the word which God has written on the brow of every man.
>
> VICTOR HUGO

finally see the city of God, and there was so much beauty that they fell sick with happiness and cried out, "If you see my Beloved, tell him I am sick with love." The city was so glorious that they could not yet look upon it directly but had to use an instrument made for that purpose. This, after all, is the dwelling place of God.

CLOSER TO GOD'S HOME

A mother asked her little daughter what she had learned in Sunday school that morning. The girl said, "We learned about a man who took long walks with God, and one day he was out walking with God and he had walked so long and so far that God said to him, 'You know, you're actually closer to My home than you are to yours, so why don't you just come and live with Me?'"

You, LORD, have delivered me from death, my eyes from tears, my feet from stumbling, that I may walk before the LORD in the land of the living.
Psalm 116:8-9

Well, perhaps Enoch's journey didn't happen exactly as this girl described, but she gave a good description of how it *might* have happened. And isn't it a wonderful thought that as we walk alongside the Lord throughout our lives we are getting closer to His heart, His home, and an eternal relationship with the Almighty? It's a beautiful image and a compelling truth. Our hearts and lives truly do draw closer to God when we walk with Him.

After my mother turned 102 years old I asked her one day on the phone, "Are you sure that when you die you are going to go to heaven?" She said, "I am so sure, it's as if I am already there." Those are the words of a woman who knows that her walk with God leads to a destination.

HELP FOR THE JOURNEY

Usually when I go to the airport, I have a confirmed ticket, but sometimes I've flown standby. When I go standby I am nervous, waiting anxiously, not knowing if I will hear my name over the intercom. With a confirmed ticket, I am relaxed in the terminal lounge, assured that I have a seat waiting for me on the plane.

If you believe that Jesus is the Son of God and have trusted Him as your personal sin-bearer, then this is what you can expect to inherit in the life to come. As you will discover, our destiny includes sitting on the throne of the universe next to Jesus. Please pay special attention to the phrases in italics.

- Through faith in Christ, you can have a confirmed ticket, knowing today that your place in heaven is secured. Enoch had assurance before he disappeared that he knew God and was pleasing to Him. By faith in God's promises and by walking the following steps, we can be assured of the same.
  - Delight in and rest in the power of the resurrection
  - Transfer your trust to God
  - Experience a transformation of heart
- As you go on actual walks and take in the scenery, consider the view from your journey with God. What miracles, wonders, hopes, and transformations have filled the horizon during your lifetime? What do you still hope to see during your lifetime? What do you now hope that others will see when they reflect back on your life someday?
- If we look at my lovely mom's response to my question, it's easy to wonder, *Where does such personal assurance come from?* She has spent many years taking those important steps and resting in her fellowship with God. She has walked with God and has embraced the pleasure, rewards, and assurances of that journey.

  Has your fellowship with God waned or increased? Are you where you want to be in the faith journey? Consider what you want your walk with God to look like in the years ahead.

May you be blessed with a long life of fellowship with God, and may you too be able to respond with great joy and assurance, "I am sure."

Now faith is the assurance of things hoped for, and the conviction of things not seen.

Hebrews 11:1 NASB

ISᵉ EGADI

Marifimo I.   Levanzo I.   C.d.S.Vito   I.delle Femine   C.d.Gallo

M.Cuccio

Colombara I.   Corini   PALERMO   C.Zafarano

M.Giuliano   Monreale   Bagheria

Maritimo I.   Trapani   Partinico   Piana

Formiche I.   Castellamare   Alcamo   Termini   Termini

I.Borrone   Calatafimi   TRAPANI   Caccamo   I.di Col

I.Longa   Pantaleo   Salemi   Corleone   M.Madd

C.Boeo   Marsala   Bellice F.   PALERMO

Mazzara   Paolarina   Bisacquino   CALTA

Castelvetrano   M.Genuardo   S.Cater

Arena F.   M.Calogero   Cammarata   Villalba

GIR   Gollabellotta

P.di Sorello   Sciacca   Platani F.

C.S.Marco   GENTI

Massaoli   Cattolica   Canicatti

M A R E   C.Bianco   Girgenti   Caro

I.Nerita   Palma

(Ferdinandea)   Lic

1831.   P.S.Nicolo

L I B I C

LA

SICILIA